Timeline of Shakespeare's theatres

1576

James Burbage opens London's first theatre in Shoreditch, outside of the city limits. He names it 'The Theatre'.

1598

Burbage's acting company, 'The Lord Chamberlain's Men' are kicked out of their theatre by the owner of the land.

1597

Theatres close to try and contain the spread of the Bubonic Plague (the Black Death).

1599

The Globe Theatre is built in Bankside with money invested by the actors in Burbage's playing company and the playwright William Shakespeare.

1603

Elizabeth I dies. King James, a great lover of plays, renames the company 'The King's Men' and allows the opening of an indoor theatre, called 'Blackfriars'.

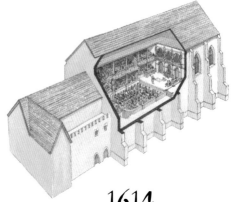

1614

'The King's Men' rebuild and reopen a second Globe theatre.

1613

The original Globe theatre burns down when a cannon sets the thatch on the roof alight.

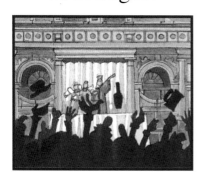

1616

William Shakespeare dies.

Layout of The Globe Theatre

Room in the roof where stage machinery kept

Gallery (where musicians or nobles could sit during the show)

Side doors

Central curtain

Stage

The Globe Theatre had a similar layout to the Coliseum in Rome, although it was much smaller. The wide side doors allowed big props such as chariots, thrones and trees to be wheeled on. A trapdoor in the stage meant that devils or ghosts could spring up from the ground during a performance, and the central curtain could also be flung back to reveal surprising plot twists.

Three trumpet blasts were given to announce the start of the play, and then the actors would stride out onto the stage. They had to try and capture the audience's attention at once, without the help of a rising curtain or dimmed lights. Music from drums, lutes, trumpets and pipes was an important element in most plays, and for the jig (a comic dance) that was performed afterwards.

Author:
Jacqueline Morley studied English at
Oxford University. She has taught English and
History, and now works as a freelance writer.
She has written historical fiction and non-fiction
for children.

Artist:
David Antram was born in Brighton, England,
in 1958. He studied at Eastbourne College of
Art and then worked in advertising for fifteen
years before becoming a full-time artist. He has
illustrated many children's non-fiction books.

Series creator:
David Salariya was born in Dundee,
Scotland. He has illustrated a wide range of books
and has created and designed many new series
for publishers in the UK and overseas. David
established The Salariya Book Company in 1989.
He lives in Brighton, England, with his wife,
illustrator Shirley Willis, and their son Jonathan.

Editor: Tanya Kant

Editorial Assistant: Mark Williams

Published in Great Britain in MMXVI by
Book House, an imprint of
The Salariya Book Company Ltd
25 Marlborough Place, Brighton BN1 1UB
www.salariya.com
www.book-house.co.uk
ISBN: 978-1-910706-47-3

S A L A R I Y A

1 3 5 7 9 8 6 4 2

A CIP catalogue record for this book is available
from the British Library.

Printed and bound in China.

Visit our website at **www.book-house.co.uk**
or go to **www.salariya.com** for **free** electronic versions of:
You Wouldn't Want to be an Egyptian Mummy!
You Wouldn't Want to be a Roman Gladiator!
You Wouldn't Want to be a Polar Explorer!
You Wouldn't Want to sail on a 19th-Century Whaling Ship!

PAPER FROM
SUSTAINABLE
FORESTS

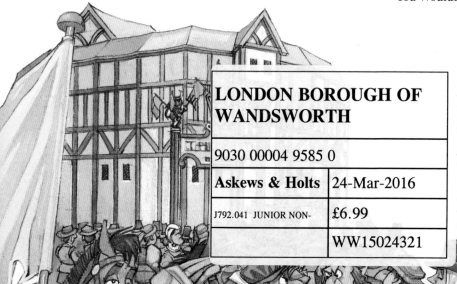

You Wouldn't Want to Be a ™
Shakespearean Actor!

Written by
Jacqueline Morley

Illustrated by
David Antram

Created and designed by
David Salariya

Some Roles You Might Not Want to Play

BOOK HOUSE

Contents

Introduction

It's 1594 and you're a young boy growing up in Shoreditch, just outside London. Until about 20 years ago, it was a quiet spot. Then, actors from the city arrived and put up a 'playhouse' there – a building just for putting on plays! Before this, players had always been travellers, setting up makeshift stages wherever they could find an audience.

Puritans (very strict Christians) like your parents don't approve of acting. They say that players are no better than beggars, asking for money for something that's not hard work – it's 'playing'. They think plays are just longer versions of the foolish shows that wandering entertainers have been putting on since medieval times. But you think your parents are wrong to say that plays are displeasing to God – they've never been to one! Well, you have (unknown to them of course), and you think plays are the best thing ever. You'd love to act in one.

▲ *Medieval entertainers*

◀ *16th-century players*

Burbage's brainwave

THE COURTYARDS of London's inns were once used for plays, but people complained about the rowdy audiences. So the London authorities banned playing in inns.

BEAR-BAITING enclosures had given Burbage an idea – build a large, round theatre, like a bear-baiting ring, with an open central yard to hold audiences.

Grrrr!

BURBAGE rented land in Shoreditch – just beyond London's city boundaries, where the ban on plays doesn't apply. He built a playhouse that could hold much bigger audiences than an inn yard.

The First theatre

In 1576 James Burbage, the manager of a company of players, opened a playhouse in Shoreditch and named it 'The Theatre'. Your parents were disgusted:'Look at all the London riffraff it's bringing here!'

But it's been a huge success. The London area now has several 'theatres' (the term has caught on), but the most exciting plays are at Burbage's. His company is now called 'The Lord Chamberlain's Men', and his son Richard is a great actor. One of the other players is a brilliant writer as well. His name is William Shakespeare.

Pick me!

No, pick me!

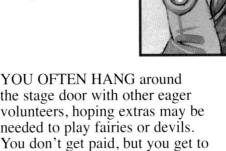

Hail!

YOU OFTEN HANG around the stage door with other eager volunteers, hoping extras may be needed to play fairies or devils. You don't get paid, but you get to see the show for free.

A BOY PLAYER has fallen sick, so a volunteer is needed – Burbage picks you! It's a small part, the fairy Moth in Shakespeare's play *A Midsummer Night's Dream*, but it's a dream come true for you.

Handy hint

Never take no for an answer! Your persistence as a volunteer has finally paid off!

The boy has talent.

BURBAGE offers you an apprenticeship but your parents say no – until they hear you get free food and lodging. They have five other children to care for, so they can't refuse.

Joining the company

Y ou soon realise theatre life is tough. As theatre owner, old James Burbage gets over half the takings. Leading company members share the rest and minor players make do on meagre wages. You're an apprentice so you get nothing – though if times are good, Richard Burbage may slip you a little money. He's training you to move and speak like a woman, so that you can play female roles. Women aren't allowed to act – it's not the proper thing to do. Young boys play the women's roles instead. When you're ready, you'll get to go on stage. Burbage will also hire you out to other companies that need boy actors.

Now is the winter of our discontent...

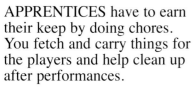

APPRENTICES have to earn their keep by doing chores. You fetch and carry things for the players and help clean up after performances.

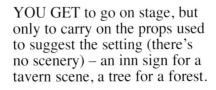

YOU GET to go on stage, but only to carry on the props used to suggest the setting (there's no scenery) – an inn sign for a tavern scene, a tree for a forest.

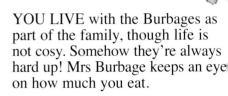

YOU LIVE with the Burbages as part of the family, though life is not cosy. Somehow they're always hard up! Mrs Burbage keeps an eye on how much you eat.

Stand up straight! Ladies never slouch!

Handy hint

When you're sweeping up after a performance, keep a sharp eye on the ground. People sometimes drop things that are worth picking up.

YOU LEARN to stay out the way of old James Burbage. He's not always good-tempered, especially if the takings are poor or if he has debts to pay.

THERE WAS a big row when Burbage's business partner accused him of stealing the company's takings. The money was kept in a box with two locks, and each partner had a key to only one lock. So neither could open the box alone. Yet money was missing!

Dirty swindler! You've copied my key!

Your big chance

Xou've been doing small parts for a while now and Richard Burbage thinks you're ready for a major role. Shakespeare has just come up with a new play – *Love's Labour's Lost*. It's sure to be a hit. You are playing the Princess of France. It's not the lead role but you have to do well! The worst part is the costume fitting – hours spent standing with tiremen (assistants who help you dress) yanking you into a metal-stiffened corset and a horrible farthingale (a metal frame that fills out your skirt).

IN YOUR ROYAL costume and wig, even your parents wouldn't recognise you.

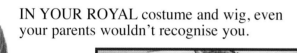

RATS ARE the tiremen's worst enemy. They've gnawed the hem of the cloak that you'll be wearing. You're sent out to buy some copper lace to patch it up.

FOR GOING OUTSIDE the theatre in costume, you get a whacking fine. Costumes are often the cast-offs of real nobles, and are very valuable – so don't damage yours!

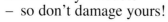

To avoid making a sensational unplanned appearance, practise walking in your skirt and heels.

Corset

Farthingale

15

A working day

After morning rehearsals, the leading players gather to hear Shakespeare read from his latest play – it's called *Romeo and Juliet*. He reads out some lines and they sound good, so the company decides to buy the play. You can't believe your luck when Shakespeare suggests you play Juliet. It will really launch your career.

But your big break makes life difficult. Boys who've been acting longer than you are jealous, and learning such a big part is an awful lot of work. You've got some long days ahead of you.

This is not very ladylike!

YOU WAKE UP feeling chilly – the Burbages' attic is far from warm. Last night you were much too tired to study your part for today's rehearsal. Better skip breakfast and learn it now.

YOU LOSE TRACK of time trying to learn your lines and old Burbage catches you coming in late. Now you'll get no pocket money – he'll say it went to pay the fine for lateness.

DURING rehearsal you muddle up two speeches. It doesn't help that it's been raining. The stage is open to the sky and now the floor is slippery. You keep sliding all over the place!

But soft, what light through yonder window breaks? It is the east, and Juliet is the sun!

Handy hint
There's no such thing as a free lunch. If James Burbage treats the players to a meal, he pays himself back from their share of the takings.

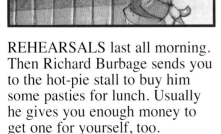

I'll have two large and one extra small.

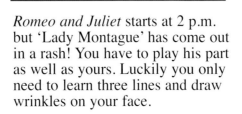

You're on in five minutes!

REHEARSALS last all morning. Then Richard Burbage sends you to the hot-pie stall to buy him some pasties for lunch. Usually he gives you enough money to get one for yourself, too.

Romeo and Juliet starts at 2 p.m. but 'Lady Montague' has come out in a rash! You have to play his part as well as yours. Luckily you only need to learn three lines and draw wrinkles on your face.

TONIGHT the players are giving a private performance. Sometimes you play for Queen Elizabeth but this time it's for law students. They're very rowdy – you long for bed!

17

Stretching your memory

You're a star player now, the company's first choice for female leads. But there's a downside to success. You're up till midnight, learning lines until you feel your head will split.

The trouble is, to keep the audiences coming, the company performs a different play each day. It can have up to 40 plays on the go and you must act in all of them. You have to remember every part you've ever learned! About 15 plays a year will be new; the rest are revivals of old plays. In some you play more than one role, so altogether you need to keep at least 50 parts in your head. Minor actors who play many parts may need to memorise 100 roles.

COMPANIES pay writers to churn out plays. Most do a rough job for little money. Your company is lucky to have Shakespeare writing for it.

EACH PLAY'S text (known as its 'book') must be checked by the Office of the Master of the Revels. They make sure there's nothing in it that might offend the Queen.

IF A PLAY is a hit, its text becomes valuable. It's locked away so rival companies can't use it. Watch out for men in the audience taking notes – they may be making a pirated version.

You'll love this one.

O Romeo, Romeo...
I can barely keep my
eyes open...

Handy hint
Parts are easier to
learn if they're
in a tragic play.
Tragedies are
mostly in verse
and the rhythm
makes lines more
memorable.

THE BOOKKEEPER is
crucial to a successful
performance. He stands
backstage and ensures that
everything runs smoothly.
In his book he notes each
player's moves, as well as
the props and sound effects
required. If your mind
goes blank, he's there to
prompt you.

Two bangs
and then exit
stage left.

19

The plague

Each summer, Londoners dread the return of a deadly illness known as the plague. Victims get a sudden fever and many die a couple of days later. No-one knows what causes the plague, but every few years it arrives with the summer heat and seems to get passed on rapidly in crowds. Theatres draw the largest crowds, so they are shut down during bad outbreaks.

This year, you've seen red crosses painted on doors, warning people of the places that are plague-stricken. Every night, death carts rumble through the streets, picking up the bodies that have been left on doorsteps. It won't be long before playgoing is banned.

IN THE HOUSE of a plague victim, no-one is allowed out. You bring food to trapped relatives.

PEOPLE say bad air causes the plague. Bonfires are lit in the hope that they will purify the air. No-one yet knows that the disease is actually caught from fleas carried by black rats.

SO MANY people have died that proper funerals are not possible. Bodies are piled into pits and sprinkled with powdered limestone to hide the smell.

PLAYERS' wagons join the queues of Londoners trying to escape the plague. But the players are not just fleeing disease – they are seeking work, too.

21

On the road

PUBLICITY is essential. You need to let everyone in town know you've arrived. The whole company parades through the streets, making as much din as possible.

When the theatres are shut, players have to travel – just as they did in the old days. It's not good news for anyone. Audiences in towns and villages will be small, especially if people fear you're bringing the plague with you. Managers need to keep costs down and many men get the sack. You job is safe because the company always needs 'women'. But living on reduced pay – and sleeping in barns or underneath the wagon – makes you think you'd be better off at home.

PLAYERS CAN'T perform without permission from the local mayor. The first town you visit is so afraid of the plague that the mayor pays you to go away.

YOU HAVE better luck in the next town. The mayor pays for the first performance and invites important townsfolk to be his guests. He even gives the company a free meal.

DURING the mayor's meal, some of the more rowdy players get into a brawl. They end up spending a day in the stocks.

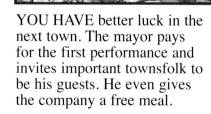

NOW ALL the players have a bad reputation. Somehow it seems to travel ahead of you. At the next village you are turned away.

Christmas crisis

It's 1598 and you've had a terrible year. Old Burbage passed away in 1597, and the company has been thrown out of the Theatre. The owner of the land it's built on is claiming that the Theatre is his. He says the Burbages were such bad tenants that they've lost their right to it. The players are fuming, so they've arranged to have the Theatre dismantled secretly over Christmas. They're going to take its valuable timbers (wooden beams) and build a new playhouse elsewhere! But as the players start dismantling, officials arrive with a writ (written command), ordering the players to stop. But instead a fight starts!

The company was thrown out of the Theatre over a year ago. Since then it's been using a downmarket theatre called the Curtain. You made a big impression there in Shakespeare's *Much Ado About Nothing*.

THE FIGHT has not helped Richard Burbage's temper. Like father, like son!

THE TIMBER RAID gives the company what it needs – essential building materials. It has them carted to another site to build a new theatre.

The Globe

The company has a new theatre now, across the river Thames in an area called Bankside. It's called the Globe. Even using the old timbers, it's cost a lot to build. The leading players put up the money for it, so the Globe is owned by them, not by a manager. Shakespeare is an investor, which means you're acting in his theatre now. You love life on Bankside. Londoners come here for the taverns, the bear-baiting and the theatres. Being south of the river means Bankside is outside city control, so anything goes!

THE GLOBE is similar in plan to the Theatre, but grander. People pay a single penny to stand in the yard, two to sit in the galleries and three for good seats with cushions.

THE CROWD in the yard are called the groundlings. They don't mind standing, but if they dislike the play they'll throw things at you. Let's hope it's only apple cores and nutshells.

'GATHERERS' collect the entrance money (there are no tickets). Some scratch their ears a lot. Are they stealing money by slipping coins down their necks?

Gable

Thatched roof

Gallery

Stage

Staircase

Yard
(standing area)

Backstage at the Globe

The years are passing, and for a boy player like you, time is your enemy. You're now too old to play Juliet. These days you play her mother. Backstage in the tiring house – the place where players get into their attire (costumes) – your mirror tells you that you're losing that fragile look. Soon you'll be eighteen and too masculine for female parts.

All around you people are rushing about, looking for props, tweaking costumes and calling for the trumpeter to signal the start of the performance. You're no longer the centre of attention.

BAD WEATHER sometimes means performances have to be cancelled. Londoners watch to see if the flag's flying above the theatre (right). If it is, there'll be a show.

THE GLOBE'S stairway leads to the stage gallery and the storerooms. Here there is a pulley that lowers actors playing gods onto the stage from the heavens.

This flag shows that the weather is good enough for a performance.

Handy hint

Avoid mistakes by checking the 'plot' before you go on. It's an outline of the day's play.

I'm going to need more make-up.

Fire!

It's 1613 – two decades since you first joined the players. Let's face it, your career has not been a success. The company has made it clear that you're not cut out to be a male lead. Today you have a walk-on part as an attendant to Cardinal Wolsey in Shakespeare's *Henry VIII*.

In this scene, the king and his followers have just arrived at Wolsey's feast, disguised as shepherds. The stagehands fire a real cannon, placed in the gable at the top of the theatre, to salute the king's approach. While everyone else is looking at the stage, you are so bored that you're staring into space. So you are the first one to notice that the roof is in flames!

Gable

Bang!

I don't remember that line...

I want my money back!

THE THEATRE is full. Well over 2,000 people head for the doors. There are only two exits, but somehow everyone manages to get out unharmed.

THE ONLY PERSON to suffer is a man whose breeches catch fire. Luckily he has just bought himself a drink, so he puts it to good use.

WHEN THE CANNON was fired, some sparks or smouldering wadding must have landed on the roof and set the thatch alight. Once the fire gets going, nothing can stop it.

Fire!

Handy hint

To prevent fire, rebuild the Globe with a tiled roof, not a thatched one.

THERE'S GALLONS of water on hand in the river Thames, but the only way to get it to the fire is to pass buckets. (Professional firefighting with pumps is a thing of the future.)

IN TWO HOURS, the Globe is burned to the ground. The company decides to rebuild it at once. It reopens in 1614.

31

A roof over your head

The company's fortunes are growing. Queen Elizabeth died in 1603, and the new king loves plays even more than she did. King James has renamed the company 'The King's Men' and it has been allowed to open a theatre in the city. It's called Blackfriars – the first indoor theatre in London. The company plays there in the winter and at the Globe in the summer.

For you the future's not so rosy. You only get the old-man roles. You weren't bad as Polonius in *Hamlet*. If you had known things would turn out this way, would you still have wanted to be a Shakespearean actor?

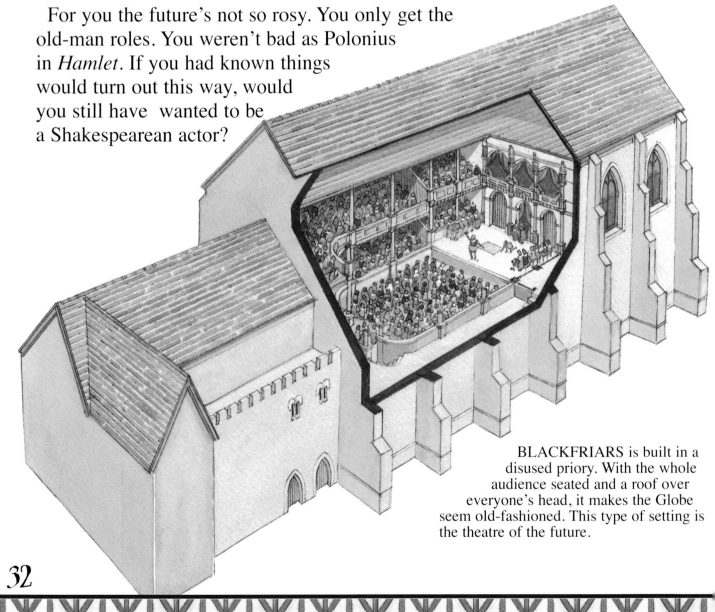

BLACKFRIARS is built in a disused priory. With the whole audience seated and a roof over everyone's head, it makes the Globe seem old-fashioned. This type of setting is the theatre of the future.

Handy hint

No need to bellow your lines at Blackfriars. In a smaller space, you need a subtler acting style.

This above all: to thine own self be true.

Fie, Polonius, that's acting most foul!

BLACKFRIARS draws a rich audience. The fops who sit in the best seats at the side of the stage like to show off their fine clothes and make irritating comments.

INDOOR theatres need candles. The play stops while they are trimmed, to keep them from going out. (This is how the custom of intervals began.)

Glossary

Apprentice An unpaid trainee who serves his master for a fixed number of years in return for training.

Apprenticeship The position that an apprentice takes.

Attire Clothing, especially a costume.

Bear-baiting The so-called 'sport' of watching dogs fight against a chained bear. Bear-baiting was banned in England in 1835.

Bookkeeper In the Shakespearean theatre, a supervisor who noted players' moves and gave directions.

Breeches An outer leg-garment for men, popular in the 16th century, reaching from the waist to just below the knee.

Company A group of entertainers that perform together.

Cutpurse A thief who cut the straps of the money purses that people in 16th-century England hung from their belts.

Doublet A man's short, snug-fitting jacket, popular in the 16th century.

Farthingale A framework of cane or metal hoops that filled out a woman's skirt.

Gable The triangular part of a wall between the slopes of the roof.

Lord Chamberlain's Men The company of players formed in 1594 and later known as the King's Men, which included William Shakespeare and Richard Burbage.

Master of the Revels The official in charge of organising royal entertainments and licensing plays.

Player The 16th-century term for an actor.

Playhouse A 16th-century term for a theatre.

Pomander A mixture of sweet-smelling spices formed into a ball, often kept in a pierced metal holder hung around the neck.

Priory A kind of monastery, whose leader is called a prior. Monasteries were put to other uses after Henry VIII abolished them in the 1530s.

Props Objects used in a play, such as weapons or furniture.

Puritans Members of a Christian group, who led a life of strict simplicity, based on Biblical teaching.

Rogue A dishonest or troublesome person.

Stage door The door at the rear of a theatre, by which the actors enter it.

Stage gallery A balcony area above the stage that was used by the actors during performances, or by musicians playing music as part of the show.

Stocks A wooden frame with holes in it, used to hold people by their ankles. Stocks were set up in public so prisoners could be humiliated by other townspeople.

Takings The money received from the audience for a play.

Thatch A straw-like material traditionally used to cover roofs.

Tiremen Assistants who helped actors put on their costumes.

Tiring house An area behind the stage where players got ready, and where costumes and props were stored.

Tragedies Plays that deal with serious subjects and have an unhappy ending.

Trim (of candles) To remove melted wax and cut the wick of a candle so that it will not make too much smoke.

Wadding A piece of cloth that was rammed into a cannon to hold the gunpowder and cannonball in place.

Walk-on part A role which does not involve speaking.

Writ A written command, issued by a court.

Index

The audience

Going to a play, especially a new one, was a major excitement. It appealed to everyone from courtiers and rich city merchants to the poorest craftsmen and labourers.

A rich lord and lady would have sat in the best sections of seating, known as the lords' rooms, which were closest to the stage. Foreign ambassadors and high-ranking nobles expected to be given a seat in the musicians' gallery.

Gentlewomen of a well-to-do family who wished to see a play had to be accompanied by a man. This was a sign that they were respectable and not to be spoken to by anyone who did not know them. A male servant was enough for this purpose.

People who stood in the theatre yard were called groundlings. Respectable shopkeepers and their families rubbed shoulders with household servants, fishwives, soldiers, seamen, poor artisans and workmen of all kinds.

There were no tickets for performances so people who wanted a good view came early. There was often a lot of jostling to get in – the ideal opportunity for cutpurses to get to work. There were lots of them in the crowd.

Theatre before Shakespeare

1000 BC The ancient Greeks honoured Dionysus, god of wine and fertility, in a festival of wild dancing. During the following centuries, dance-drama became part of these festivals.

6th century BC By this time, the festivities for Dionysus had become formal ceremonies of dance and song performed by a chorus of 50 men. Prizes were given for the best song.

534 BC Thespis, a priest of Dionysus, is said to be the first person ever to appear on stage as an actor playing a part in a play. Another word for actor, 'thespian', comes from his name.

500 BC Outdoor theatres were developed, with tiers of wooden seating for audiences and a special performance area. Over time, stone seating was provided for the audiences at these ceremonies.

27 BC onwards Roman theatres in the Roman Empire, modelled on those of Greece, staged increasingly extravagant and violent entertainments.

312 AD The Roman Emperor Constantine was converted to Christianity. Laws were passed banning cruel entertainments.

1264 AD Pope Urban IV established the church festival of Corpus Christi in June of this year. It soon became popular throughout Europe to put on performances of religious plays as a way to celebrate the festival.

15th – 16th centuries AD Meanwhile, professional troupes of travelling entertainers were developing 'interludes' (short plays) as part of their routines.

1564 AD Birth of William Shakespeare in Stratford-upon-Avon, England.